WE ALL WANT TO BE HAPPY

A BOOK OF THOUGHTS

ANN MULLEN

We All Want to Be Happy: A Book of Thoughts (Volume 1)
Published by Annmuma Publishing
Mesquite, Texas, U.S.A.

Copyright ©2024, ANN MULLEN. All rights reserved.

No part of this book may be reproduced in any form or by any mechanical means, including information storage and retrieval systems without permission in writing from the publisher/author, except by a reviewer who may quote passages in a review. All images, logos, quotes, and trademarks included in this book are subject to use according to trademark and copyright laws of the United States of America.

MULLEN, ANN, Author
WE ALL WANT TO BE HAPPY
ANN MULLEN

Library of Congress Control Number: 2024918201

ISBN: 979-8-9914644-0-6, 979-8-9914644-2-0 (paperback)
ISBN: 979-8-9914644-3-7 (hardcover)
ISBN: 979-8-9914644-1-3 (digital)

BIOGRAPHY & AUTOBIOGRAPHY / Women
SELF-HELP / Personal Growth / Happiness
BODY, MIND & SPIRIT / Inspiration & Personal Growth

Editing: Nina Marshall (jacobswc.com/team/ramadevinina@yahoo.com)
Book Design: Book Ripple Publishing (bookripple.com)
Publishing Management: Tim Jacobs (jacobswc.com)
Publishing Consulting: Susie Schaefer (finishthebookpublishing.com)

QUANTITY PURCHASES: Schools, companies, professional groups, clubs, and other organizations may qualify for special terms when ordering quantities of this title. For information, visit annmuma-publishing.com

All rights reserved by ANN MULLEN and ANNMUMA PUBLISHING. This book is printed in the United States of America.

This book is written in memory of those who taught me the meaning of love, especially my parents, John and Mary Yeager, and my life partners, Ronnie Mullen and Randall Martin. Life is good.
– Ann Mullen-Martin

FOREWORD

I hold no degrees in psychology or psychiatry. My only claim to fame is that I am happy, and I want to share some of that happiness with you.

Did you know, happiness can last forever and cannot be taken from you without your permission? However, if you suffer from depression because of a medical, emotional or mental illness, I encourage you to seek treatment from a licensed professional.

My suggestions and shared stories are intended for those who experience day-to-day upsets, trials and life's ups and downs.

There are various forms of happiness. Over my first eighty years, I have learned that we are on our own as we search for it, regardless of our beliefs, practices and understanding. There is no magic bullet. No one else can make you happy; happiness comes from within, or it does not come at all.

If no one can make you happy, then it follows we cannot make others happy. However, our shared happiness can result in collective contentment.

Fortunately, I learned this fact at my mother's knee, around the age of five or six, and I will share her knowledge in the first chapter using The Big Chief Tablet. As an outgrowth of this simple system, I've been successful in overcoming a built-in tendency to sadness to the point that many around me say I see the world via rose-colored glasses.

Not true—or maybe 'so true' in that we all see the world as we are—not as it is.

I invite you to read my stories and share my happiness.

Life is good—or, maybe, it's as good as we choose to make it.

CONTENTS

Foreword   4

CHAPTER ONE:
The Big Chief Tablet   8

CHAPTER TWO:
Living in the Now   13

CHAPTER THREE:
Addiction   15

CHAPTER FOUR:
Freedom Is a State of Mind   19

CHAPTER FIVE:
Past Waiting for the Right Time   22

CHAPTER SIX:
The Little Green Frog   27

CHAPTER SEVEN:
Have You Accomplished Your Purpose?   33

CHAPTER EIGHT:
Are You Someone's Glue?   35

CHAPTER NINE:
A Stroke of Luck   41

CHAPTER TEN:
A Vacation for Two   57

CHAPTER ELEVEN:
Coming to Grips with Getting Old   61

CHAPTER TWELVE:
Follow the String   75

CHAPTER THIRTEEN:
What Is the Greatest Evil?   81

CHAPTER FOURTEEN:
The Spoon Collection   87

CHAPTER FIFTEEN:
Memories to Take with You   92

CHAPTER SIXTEEN:
Finding Truth   95

CHAPTER SEVENTEEN:
The Boy in the Green Shirt   99

CHAPTER EIGHTEEN:
Laughter Heals   101

CHAPTER NINETEEN:
A Work in Progress   107

CHAPTER TWENTY:
Some of My Favorite Thoughts   111

CHAPTER ONE
The Big Chief Tablet

At eight years old, I had the blues.

I was laying on a quilt in the side yard, reading a book and looking at the clouds. I had no good reason to be sad, but I felt desperately alone. A tear rolled down my cheek as I ran inside to Mama, who welcomed me with a hug.

"You know, Olevia, I don't know why you get so sad. You have everything to be happy about. Do you still have your Big Chief Tablet?"

"I don't know either, Mama. I just don't even want to be here." Tears fell in earnest, and Mama gave me a huge hug. This was not Mama's first run-in with my sad sessions, but, to my memory, that's the day the Big Chief Tablet first became a tool.

I suppose if it had not been the early fifties, and if I had not lived in rural Central Louisiana, I would have been into 'counseling' somewhere.

"Okay, Olevia. Open your tablet."

I did. "And what?" I studied the page and looked up at her. This new approach got my attention.

"At the very top of your page, I want you to write down something that makes you happy. Can you think of anything that would make you smile, right this minute?"

"An ice cream cone, especially strawberry." I started to get into the game between sniffles.

"Well, let's write that down. It makes me smile too. What else do you have?"

"Nothing! Mama, I'm sad!" My frustration spilled over, and tears fell in torrents.

Mama calmly continued, "Okay, let's see if I can do one for you. What about Grunt? Does he make you smile?"

Grunt was my dog; he earned his name because, since puppyhood, he would often grunt in his sleep.

"Yeah, I guess Grunt can make me smile." And I did, as I thought of him.

"I promise to talk about what makes you sad if you promise to list as many things as you can that make you smile."

I accepted Mama's challenge as she returned to the kitchen to begin preparing dinner. By the time she came to check on me, things that made me smile covered the entire page.

Together, we read every entry and amplified each one of them through questions and remembering why they made me happy. By the time we finished, I was not only no longer sad, but had a new focus.

On that day, I learned that sometimes, happiness is a matter of perspective. I learned to count my blessings before I considered the chuckholes in my life.

That encounter with The Big Chief Tablet turned out to be the first of many, and maybe not even the most memorable.

****

A conversation with my mom when I was eleven:

"I want you to get well."

"So do I, baby, and maybe I will. But, if I don't, that's not the road we're on. We must walk the paths chosen for us, or maybe by us, before we begin life's journey. But I promise wherever those paths go, they will be filled with good things special for us, you and me."

"But everybody's mama's not dying. It's not fair!" I wanted sympathy, not explanations. I learned that sometimes what we think we want is not what we need.

"Well, maybe if I had gotten a long path, you wouldn't be my little girl. I wouldn't like that. Would you?"

"No!"

"Then I guess we're pretty lucky, aren't we?" She chuckled and gave me a little squeeze. "We still have a lot of living to do and a lot more fun to have."

I loved spending time with my Mama and her precious wisdom.

I learned a couple of things:

- We are each on a path of our choosing
- It's up to us to watch for and understand our blessings in comparison to our lessons and our trials.

****

Mama's gift helped me overcome the sadness that remains a built-in part of my psyche.

I did not completely unwrap this valuable gift during those childhood sessions. As life would have it, paths have chuckholes. I mentally brought out, and still do bring out, The Big Chief Tablet when sadness starts to cloud my sunny days. It continues to comfort me as I explore more and more layers of this most cherished and precious gift.

CHAPTER TWO
Living in the Now

Dreams should be! But what should they be?

Many of us find ourselves too busy making a living and doing the necessary daily things to care for our families to contemplate dreams. We have some vague plans of what we want to do someday, if we are blessed to make it to that someday.

What we don't always remember is today is someday. We are frequently living our dreams while wondering if we can reach our dreams.

Too often, we think of our dreams as something to come, like traveling, owning our home, accomplishing some goal, etc. When life becomes heavy, I find the load lightened by remembering my dreams of some years ago.

For example, my dreams at age nineteen might have included getting married, having a family, getting a job, finishing my education, etc.

If I had taken the time to remember past dreams at age thirty, I would have found those dreams had come to pass; I was living my dreams. Of course, I had new dreams of raising my family successfully, taking a family vacation to Colorado, buying a home, and so forth.

When I'm bored or wondering about the why of today, I am reminded to live in the now, be cognizant of the dreams accomplished and keep busy filling the hopper, so to speak, with new ones.

Now is all I have, and it is my responsibility not to waste a minute in regret for the past or longing for the future.

Dreams should be lived and relished on a day-to-day basis.

CHAPTER THREE
Addiction

Addiction takes many forms. What are you addicted to? I'm talking about those little quirks we have within ourselves.

There are habits, both good and bad, that could be more accurately described as mental and emotional addictions. Some work toward personal peace, contentment and prosperity, while others are poisonous to healthy living.

Take the person who always replies to the question: "How are you today" with something like, "I'm okay, except for a little ache in my knee." That person may have an addiction to being ill. So, they share a little ache to make their world more normal for them.

We all know people who cannot just report a good time when asked how their weekend was. You'll get an answer something like: "Great, but my hair appointment was delayed fifteen minutes and wasted half my morning."

That person may be addicted to complaining and is more comfortable in a world where not everything goes as planned.

Some individuals are addicted to losing. In some instances, losing served them well, as in the case of an undisciplined or unmotivated child. That child slides by in life, never learning the joy of responsibility or the joy of winning through their own efforts.

Some individuals were brainwashed by a parent, a teacher, a spouse, or someone they considered an authority figure. Perhaps a tendency to being clumsy was reinforced by jokes or a nickname. As a result, they come to feel they are clumsy and second best to their peers. They may fall into an addiction with inferiority.

We should work toward becoming addicted to winning, to being satisfied, contented, pleasant and a contributing member of society. We don't have the right to blame our lack of progress on society or on limited physical or mental capacity.

Countless people excel worldwide, despite personal, physical or mental limits.

Some are well-known, such as Leonardo da Vinci, Sir Isaac Newton, or Helen Keller. Most names are unknown outside their immediate circle or profession, such as Dr. Ruth Pitts, an accomplished pianist and teacher with only five fingers between two hands.

There is a statute of limitations—or should be—on using any abuse or circumstance as an excuse for an addiction to a second-class life. Breaking the patterns and the strings tying us to our discontent is difficult but doable.

The focus of our dependence must be the right thoughts.

Where's that Twelve Step Plan?

What you think upon grows!

CHAPTER FOUR

Freedom Is a State of Mind

We make a choice, every hour of every day, to be happy or not. The circumstances change, but we control how we manage them.

That may sound a bit like Pollyanna, but it is not. I've had my share of losses, including being unexpectedly widowed twice.

The first occurred days before our fortieth anniversary, while walking down a path and planning a celebration. The second followed fourteen years of marriage that ended with Covid. My mom crossed over before my thirteenth birthday. Yet, I know I have been blessed beyond my wildest dreams. But what part of these experiences can be cast as freedom?

Again, it depends on what we focus on: the loss or the good memories we never have to relinquish. We have the freedom to choose.

Recently, I engaged in a conversation with a friend of mine on the question: "What does freedom really feel like?"

We each pondered it a while and ultimately came to the same conclusion. It took some debate to get there. My first thought compared the feeling of freedom to hearing the final bell ring on the last day of grammar school. Long, lazy summer days, laying on a quilt on the lawn, just looking at the clouds, reading, thinking about anything and everything. To me, that was perfect freedom.

So, does freedom require the ability to do nothing?

My friend's position was that freedom walks hand-in-hand with education. We agreed that education involves more than book-learning; awareness and enlightenment, acquired by living a life of curiosity in search of wisdom increases one's freedom.

An open mind allows greater opportunity for liberty. Knowledge frees an individual from their own misconceptions, intolerances, prejudices and fears. A tolerant, non-prejudiced person is allowed to love, not only themselves, but others, with all the warts and shortcomings we share. Only with the ability to truly love, can one's soul and spirit experience true freedom.

At the end of our conversation, we agreed it is possible true freedom cannot be experienced in our human condition. Perhaps, it will only be upon hearing the very last bell to ring that we know true and complete freedom.

For now, we see through a glass darkly, and our best hope is to enjoy each pocket of emancipation as it comes.

CHAPTER FIVE

Past Waiting for the Right Time

Several years ago, while birding at Dry Tortugas Island in Florida, I met a man who caused me to re-think my life. I had my bird book and binoculars, while my husband had his binoculars and camera equipment. We were taking a break on a park bench discussing our day's successes.

A man, about forty or so, began setting up his camera on a tripod. While Randall was a fledgling birder, he had taken to the wing many years ago when it came to photography. The sight of good camera equipment, as well as a fellow shutterbug, got his juices flowing. He began a conversation.

"What kind of camera is that?"

"It's a Canon with a three-hundred lens on it. Is that a Canon EOS Rebel you have there? Looks like a step or two above mine."

"It's the Rebel. Just got it a couple of weeks before we started this trip. So far, I like it. Do you use a stabilizer?"

"I do anytime I use a three-hundred or more lens."

"I'm with you. That's a nice tripod."

"Well, here on the Island, we've gotten some real good looks at peregrines and broad-winged hawks. They'll sit for quite a while. I'm hoping to get a shot of one today."

Have you ever used a telescope with your camera?"

"No. What do you mean?"

"I bought one equipped with a camera attachment. I've gotten some striking moon shots."

"That's pretty expensive, isn't it? I'm afraid it's going to have to wait until I'm a little further down the road."

Randall replied, "I guess I'm already further down that road. If life were a football game, I'm pretty sure I'm in the fourth quarter."

Two of the three of us laughed. The man was not sure whether he should laugh or apologize. "I didn't mean that. I wasn't referring to your age. I just..."

"No offense taken. It's true. I'm past waiting for the right time."

"Well, as long as the game's not on the line yet, I guess all is okay."

They continued to talk about lenses, *f-stops,* megapixels, etc. until someone spotted a Cape May warbler, and our attention changed focus. After a few minutes, the guy went one way, and we wandered off in another direction, but that conversation continued to haunt me.

I have been blessed or cursed (depends on who you ask) by my personal philosophy of life. My kids and co-workers tease me by saying I live in *Ann Land,* where I expect things to always go well. They usually do, and I typically do not get caught up in worrying about the future.

My approach is: if the rent's paid, the groceries bought, and you have any money left, then buy it, rent it, or experience it. I am aware of my responsibility to take care of my tomorrows, but I cannot, or will not, do so at the peril of today.

I'm convinced our individual assignments are to live as if we had forever—because we do, in some sense of forever—and to live as if today were our last, because it may be in another sense of that forever. Those are not mutually exclusive goals, but rather two sides of the same goal.

In the real world, there is no further down the road.

CHAPTER SIX
The Little Green Frog

Finding contentment in a world of discontent is a never-ending goal and search.

For me, the pursuit of satisfaction with my life has taken many twists and turns. Today, I still temporarily lose my footing and flounder about, much as a sailor who has fallen from his ship or had one drink too many.

My life preserver consists of the little things, the small happenings, the old memories and life's lessons learned long ago. I invite you to share with me a brief look at what constitutes contentment to me.

The receptionist interrupted my concentration, saying, "Ann, Bob Mathers is here."

"Who?"

"The Litchfield Company rep."

"What's he doing here? It's Monday morning. You know I don't see reps on Mondays."

"He said he has an appointment, one made directly with you."

"Well, he didn't, and I'm .... uh-oh, it's on my calendar. I just don't have time today."

"What do you want me to tell him?" Alice stood her ground with no intention of coming to my rescue.

"Oh, for God's sake, Alice, just show him in. I'll give him five minutes, and that's it."

Bob walked in and smiled. "Hey, Ann. Guess you forgot about talking with me last week." Bob laughed as we shook hands. "These walls are thin. That five minutes will be enough for me."

"Oh, I'm sorry, Bob. I've just got so much to do this morning, and I never, ever make Monday morning appointments with anyone. Well, I guess I do, sometimes."

We both chuckled as I gestured for him to take a seat.

"No. I know you're really busy, and to tell the truth, we have a new agent I wanted to see this morning. He said he would be in the office only until ten. I'll give him a call and let you off the hook."

Bob dug around in his briefcase to get the flyers, brochures and gimme pens he routinely passed out to agents. "Here you go. Just keep that business coming, and if you need anything, give me a call."

We shook hands again, and as he turned to leave, he reached into his pocket.

"Oh, Ann, I'd like you to have this." He held out a tiny, green, plastic frog.

"What is it?"

"It's a plastic frog!" He grinned one of those gotcha smiles.

"I can see that!"

"I carry one of these in my pocket at all times as a reminder that I'm not in charge."

"Yeah?" I reached for the dime store trinket. "Bob, you might want to take a minute for a cup of coffee to clear your head."

He smiled again. "I'm serious about this. F-R-O-G. When it gets hectic or I'm in a jam, I reach for my frog. Fully Rely on God. Chintzy, isn't it? But it works for me."

He left, and I set that frog on top of my computer. It sits there still, today, and that scene took place twenty or more years ago. I must have glanced at that little piece of green plastic thousands of times since then, and it never fails to restore peace in my heart.

It works as a redirection device for me, a reminder of what is and isn't important, and what I can and cannot control. It keeps me centered when the world is askew. A plastic frog that I got because I made a scheduling error hops to my rescue on a regular basis to restore peace and contentment.

Peace and contentment are both elusive and readily at hand, if we know where to look. Sometimes I'm at my wits' end, and I'll get an e-mail from someone, maybe a silly little something that makes me smile or a special quote. I'm re-centered. Other times, a rainbow or a walk, some glimpse of Mother Nature at her best restores contentment in my mind.

Other times, a rainbow, a walk, or a glimpse of Mother Nature at her best restores contentment.

One day last week, I happened to see a photo of my great-granddaughter that reminded me life goes on, with or without my angst. I can get on board and share the good stuff, or I can stand at the side and complain about my misfortunes.

Contentment comes from deep inside. Much like happiness, one doesn't find it with or get it from someone else. It is self-contained yet connected to so much more. All of us are born with a seed that can, properly nurtured, grow into contentment. Being loved for who we are at the earliest ages can be the first fertilizer and root stimulator to make our search easier. Still, that seed will grow with our own nurturing efforts. I learned at an early age dream must be tethered with thankfulness and appreciation of the blessings enjoyed.

In my small town and Baptist church, everyone I knew spent time reading their Bible. I was taught that the answers to all the 'whys' in life could be found there.

Recently, while working on a *New York Times* crossword, I reached for my Bible in search of an answer to a clue. It occurred to me how my Bibles have changed over the years.

As a teenager, I underlined in red ink all the verses I thought most appropriate to me. As a young adult, I switched to a highlighter when I bought a new Bible.

Different verses now caught my attention, and I heard different messages. About thirty-five years ago, I bought a large print version, and I no longer write in my Bible. In fact, I rarely read it at all now, though I keep it next to my bed. Much like that little, green frog, I now just glance at it and feel the tension disappear.

I've added more religious reading to my search for spiritual peace. In addition to Christian-based works, I spent some time investigating and reading Muslim, Buddhist, Hindu, and Jewish writings. I've discovered there is more common ground among the world's faiths than disparity. That knowledge comforts me and adds to my personal contentment. I believe someday the world will emphasize love and tolerance over a *my-way's-better-than-yours* approach to solving our problems.

Life is endless, and this earthly existence is a mere parenthesis in a never-ending quest for knowledge and growth toward a more perfect love and intelligence. I've learned that sorrows are offset by blessings, that hurts are medicated by friends' presence and death is not real.

I'm satisfied with my journey, and that is contentment.

CHAPTER 7

Have You Accomplished Your Purpose?

I shared coffee every weekday morning with my friend, Joan, for almost forty years before she crossed over, several years ago, but I think of her often and of the many things we learned from each other.

We'd been there for each other during those times that were less than bright, as well as the shared celebrations. We'd reared children, lost loved ones, and she had a bout with breast cancer as we'd traveled through the day-to-day things that make life what it is. No subject was taboo, and we learned from the exchange of ideas.

One crossed my mind today: the why of living.

Life's good, and I enjoy getting up in the morning, but there is the question of why I have that opportunity when so many seem to pass on far before they reach their eightieth birthday. My children are grown, my grandchildren are adults, and I am alone again. I am not an activist or serving any obvious greater good by being here. I haven't marched, in protest or support of anything, since nineteen-sixty-one. I just relish every day, and sometimes ponder my blessed situation.

Why am I still here? Do I have an unaccomplished goal to work toward? I still have some things I want to do, but nothing that really affects the world. After lots of thought and reading, I concluded that life is like being a mosquito perched on a Rembrandt painting. You can't see enough of it to make sense of it.

Life can only be lived one day at a time, and each day offers choices. Our challenge is to choose what makes the world a better place to live and follow that still small voice.

Joan and I came up with our own easy answers:

- If you are still alive, you haven't yet accomplished your purpose in life!
- Grow and blossom where you are planted and once the bloom is gone, you'll cross over.

CHAPTER EIGHT

Are You Someone's Glue?

Some years back, I met a woman for dinner; she would soon be my sister-in-law, but at the time we knew little about each other. Conversation, while not stilted, consisted largely of inquiring about each other's lives. During that chat, my new friend shared a story about The Girlfriend Club.

The club consisted of a group of eight or nine women who had known each other since grade school and continued to share their lives through marriages, children, divorces, deaths—all the minutia of living. They met once a month to recharge their batteries, support each other and refocus their friendships.

I asked about their most recent get-together, and her eyes teared up. "Jackie died almost two years ago, and since then, my friends began to drop out. One called to say she had too much 'on her plate'. Another always has something else more important to do that night. One who had never missed a get together said she's traveling a lot now, and her calendar is full.

I replied, "Yeah, I've seen that in a lot of things. One person does all the organizing and planning, while everyone else simply rides the bandwagon."

She went on to explain further, "It was more than that. Jackie was fun to be around and always had something special planned—or so it seemed. Even when we took turns deciding what to do, no matter what was chosen, Jackie became animated about it. Her cancer diagnosis did not prevent her from having fun and sharing that fun with friends. We all wanted to get together because Jackie was there."

She paused for a few minutes and then said the most meaningful thing I heard that night.

"It's as if Jackie was the glue that kept us together."

That sentence has stuck in my mind ever since. As I've thought about it, I've come to realize that being glue can happen spur of the moment and can apply to situations between strangers. I remember times I stood on the precipice of falling apart and someone took the time to apply the necessary adhesive to mend the wound. These were people, living their lives, who happened to cross paths with me and could have kept walking, but didn't.

Zora, the owner of Zora's Liquor Store on the corner of Oak Lawn and Maple Avenue in Dallas, was one of those people. I had not been in Dallas long, and I passed her store everyday walking to and from work. Until November 12th, 1962, I never glanced in that direction or paid any attention as to who was there.

On that afternoon, things were different. I had turned nineteen the day before, and I had no money with three days left before payday. The air felt chilly, the sun had fallen behind the horizon and the cupboards in my apartment were bare. I began to question my decision to move to Dallas, and tears were near the surface as I approached the liquor store. Zora stood in the doorway, but I did not see her; just heard a voice:

"How's it going today?"

"Okay." I kept walking, but the tears brimmed over.

"Hey, have you got a minute? I've seen you come by the store often."

I tried to regain my composure as I turned in her direction.

I stopped, and she took out a cigarette. "Do you smoke?"

"Yes, but I'm out of cigarettes."

I now crumbled into a basket case, but she acted as if everything was okay as she handed me a pack of Marlboros.

"Here you go. You want to sit down for a couple of minutes? It's lonely out here today." She smiled, pulled up another stool from behind the counter.

I sat down. I do not remember what we talked about. My memory is limited to how I felt when I left with a pack of cigarettes and five dollars. I know I must have poured out my heart and my fears, but I have no idea of any particulars other than the feeling of peace when I walked away. That feeling can best be expressed by Christopher Robin in *Winnie the Pooh*: "You are braver than you believe, stronger than you seem and smarter than you think."

On payday, I returned the five dollars, and I don't recall ever having another conversation with Zora. I waved when I saw her in the store, and she returned my greetings. Sometimes I stopped to buy a pack of cigarettes, but we never became close friends.

About twenty or more years ago, I saw in the *Dallas Morning News* that she had died. As I read the obituary that included a story about the number of years her liquor store sat on that corner, I wondered if she remembered me as I did her. I doubt it. She was just living her life when she provided the glue I needed to hold my world together on November 12th, 1962.

One's philosophies are best expressed by the lives they live, rather than the words they speak. We get multiple opportunities in life to be someone's glue for the day, but it is easy to pass them up while we are lost in ourselves.

I try to watch for those opportunities and, though I know I miss many, my experience has been that being the glue is at least as gratifying as being the one in need of repair.

CHAPTER NINE
A Stroke of Luck

This is the story of a miracle that added great joy to our family.

On August 6th, 1991, Mary, my daughter, had just settled into bed and a twilight sleep when the phone rang. Mary and her husband, Dave, were foster parents and late-night phone calls, although not the norm, were not unheard of. On this night, they had only one foster child, Brandy, a little girl of six, the same age as their daughter, Jessie. The girls were sleeping soundly, and Dave was not yet home from his late shift on Transcon Motor Freight.

The phone sounded again, and Mary could not ignore it. As the fog cleared, the normal panic unleashed by an unexpected, middle-of-the-night ringing phone set in. She kicked the wastebasket as she stumbled out of bed. *Dang it! Why didn't I put that phone on the charger by my bed?*

"Hello."

"Mary, this is Clare. Did I wake you?"

Clare, a Child Protective Services worker not known for calling in the middle of the night to share good news, immediately got Mary's attention. Her calls typically meant the end of a good night's sleep, and this call resulted in many of them.

"Not really, I just turned out the light. What's up?"

"I have a baby here at a motel. He's tiny, about two months old, I think. Anyway, could you come pick him up for the night?"

"Clare, remember Samantha? I told you then I really don't want any more babies; giving them up is just too difficult."

"I know, Mary. I'm not asking you to keep him long-term, just for tonight."

"Okay, where are you? It's going to take me a while. Dave's not home, and I'll have to get someone to come stay with Jessie and Brandy."

"We're at the Post Motel on Harry Hines. Take your time. Oh, and, Mary, you might want to bring a diaper with you. And don't forget to put a car seat in the back seat. Do you have any preemie size onesies? George is small."

"I'll be there as quickly as I can with a blanket and a diaper."

Mary called a friend to come watch the girls, and she left Dave a note: *"Honey, set up the baby bed. I'm bringing George home."*

Thus, began George's life with our family. His name was George Soto—highly unusual spelling for a Hispanic George. My theory is the social worker misspelled it in the paperwork. After all, she had his birth date as June 8th, rather than June 6th, an error not discovered until a year later.

George's biological mom was well known to the CPS system. She had a troubled life, and she could not handle another baby. That night, in the motel, she reached her limit of desperation and walked out, leaving a drug-addicted two-month-old to make his own way. The hotel manager heard the baby crying and called 911.

What a stroke of luck for George and for our entire family!

I would like to say that George settled into life at Dellos' house with little or no trouble, but that did not occur. First, his drug addiction had to be overcome; in fact, Dave, Mary, Jessie and Brandy became victims of the drug fog in which George lived. Addiction ruled the family. George weighed less than five pounds, but the neighbors could hear his screams. Many twenty-four-hour days were spent holding, rocking, walking and soothing George. Jessie and Brandy became the helpers.

Jessie and Brandy quickly adapted to their roles and responded happily to all of Mary's requests.

"Get Mama a diaper for George," she called from the living room to girls who were just getting up.

"Okay. Can we have some cereal?" Jess asked,

"Yes. Get the Fruit Loops off that second shelf. Be careful. Don't spill the milk."

"Can we hold George?" Brandy asked.

"Yes, but just for a minute. You, first, Jessie, and then, Brandy, your turn. Sit still. Watch his head."

"Mama, why does he cry so much? Does he want his own mama?" Brandy, as a foster child, seemed to realize George's place in the family and compared it to hers.

"No, Brandy. He's sick, but he'll be okay. We just need to love him enough. Do you think we can do that?"

"Yes ma'am. I love him already." Brandy gave him a squeeze to prove it.

"So do I," Jessie added, along with a kiss on the forehead.

****

When Mary was exhausted from all-day childcare, Dave seemed to get his second wind upon arriving home from work. He'd take a quick shower and then sit in a rocking chair all night, holding and soothing George as he fought for normalcy.

****

At Thanksgiving, Mary and Dave decided to visit her grandmother and the rest of the Pennsylvania side of the family in Pittsburgh. By that time, the foster brood had increased by one, a four-year-old boy, but George remained the only baby. He had conquered his congenital addiction, but now he had to fight various intestinal illnesses, a result of no prenatal care and a premature birth. And while Bets, Mary's grandmother, enjoyed both Brandy and Robert, she fell in love with George.

By the evening of the first day, he was perched on her lap in the kitchen while she talked to Jessie.

"Jessie, I see you have two brothers and a sister now. How do you like that?"

"It's okay, I guess," Jessie responded. It was a new experience for her not to be the center of her grandmother's attention.

"Do you help your mom take care of George?"

"Yes. Sometimes he cries a lot. Did you know his birthday is the same day as yours, Gramma?" Jessie searched for something to bring the spotlight back to her.

"No, I didn't! Well, that just means I'll be in Texas next year, so we can have a birthday party together."

Jessie exploded into giggles, as she and Brandy began immediately to play birthday with Jessie's tea set left from Christmas.

In December, CPS decided Robert could be moved to Lubbock and would be reunited with his mother. By January, Brandy's mom's parental rights had been terminated, and a wonderful couple had applied to adopt her. By month's end, she moved to Georgia with her new family. Both situations appeared to be happy endings; indeed, with the help of Mary and Brandy's new mom, the girls began corresponding by mail.

At the CPS February review, the social worker shared some news with Mary and Dave. She arrived at nine, one morning. Once the pleasantries were exchanged, along with a couple of hugs for George, she began to explain the expected outcome for him.

"Mary, do you remember the night you picked George up?"

"I do indeed. I will never forget bringing that tiny bundle of baby in need of some loving care!"

"Do you also remember saying you were willing to keep him only a couple of days?"

Both Mary and Dave laughed. "Well, that's no longer case!" Dave replied. "He's become part of the family."

The social worker did not laugh, as though she suddenly realized her information may not be received with the enthusiasm she expected.

"Well, guys, the workings are underway to allow George to be adopted as his biological mother's drug and addictions are not likely to go away. The process of terminating her rights has begun."

Mary spoke up first. "Are our names on the list of parents to be considered?"

The worker cut the conversation short. "It's a little too early to talk about that. We'll discuss it again at next month's review."

She gathered her things, handed George back to Mary and left the house in what seemed to Mary and Dave to be a hurry. They had no need to discuss it before they made their decision. The bond with George etched deep and permanent as they shared his drug withdrawal, HIV tests and survival tenacity. As soon as they were alone again, they called Jessie into the living room

"Jessie, what do you think about George being your forever brother?" Mary asked.

"What? Are we 'doptin' him?"

"Well, we're certainly going to try," Dave said as he gave a hug.

Jessie pirouetted twice. "Yea! No more foster brother! George is gonna be my real brother."

When Mary first mentioned the above scene to me, it sounded like a slam dunk. George had lived with them since he was two months old. The parental and family bonding flourished, and Mary and Dave had a verifiable history with CPS; I was naive. George continued to have mountains to climb.

Just prior to the next monthly review, Mary called George's caseworker. She and Dave both liked Clare and she thought a heads-up phone call would benefit the situation.

"Clare, Dave and I would like to adopt George. What do you think?"

"I'm afraid that's not going to happen, Mary. George is Hispanic."

"So?"

"So, as a family caseworker, I need to look after George's best interests."

"What do you mean?"

"I'll set a meeting for you, Dave, me and Mark, George's guardian ad litem. We'll talk about things then. I'll try for two o'clock next Thursday."

Mary hung up in a state of disbelief. How could that be? That night she and Dave talked about the situation well into the wee hours of the morning. They decided not to panic, but rather to follow the procedure; perhaps, Clare just didn't have a clear picture of how much they could give to

George. Finally, the Thursday morning meeting happened.

As the four of them sat around the table, Mary and Dave accepted the challenge of adopting George as they fully realized success would take more than just hoping for the best.

"Clare, I don't understand why there should be an objection to Dave and me as George's parents."

"Mary, George is Hispanic!"

"I don't understand what you mean by that."

Clare took a deep breath and spoke as if explaining to a child.

"Mary and Dave, you guys are excellent foster parents, and I'm glad you've been here for George. But we're talking about a permanent family now. I must do what I think best. George needs to be raised by Hispanic parents. He needs to learn the culture. You cannot give him that."

"What would it take to get there? Mary and I are prepared to adopt George. What do we do now?" Dave joined the fray.

Mark slid the papers across the table and gave them instructions as to how they should be completed, and the particulars involved in applying for adoption. Clare continued to discourage the process, even completing the application.

"Dave, I cannot allow your application to be seriously considered. It is not best for George. I'm sorry."

As they walked down the hall, Mark called after them, and they boarded the elevator together.

"You need a lawyer. Carla Calibrize is among the best." He handed Dave a business card. "Call her today, before you get home is preferable. You are going to need a miracle to adopt this baby."

David shook his hand, and he and Mary called Carla from CPS's lobby. The reason Carla's reputation as a tiger in fighting for her clients—once she accepted them as clients—soon became apparent. Being between appointments when the call came in, she instructed Mary and Dave to come directly to her office. She had a list of questions a mile long, even before the necessary forms were brought out for completion. The list went something like this:

"How long have you been in the foster care system?"

"Do you have other children?"

"How does she feel about having a brother?"

"I'll need to meet her too."

"How long have you been married?"

"Do you have a support system living in town?"

"How long have you had George in your home?"

But the most important question landed near the end. "Why do you want George? He's a baby, and babies are easily adoptable. There are lots of families who want George."

"Because we love him, and we're willing to make whatever sacrifices are necessary to ensure we're the best parents we can be for George."

There were more questions, but that one answer seemed to seal the deal.

"Okay. This is not going to be easy. I know Clare, and she'll fight hard to get this baby into a Hispanic home. But I know Mark too, and he'll be a relentless fighter in George's corner whichever way he feels. That's a good thing. Do either of you speak Spanish?"

"No."

"Are either of you willing to learn?"

Dave spoke up first. "I've been practicing a little with the guys at work. I'll sign up immediately for a conversational Spanish class at Eastfield."

"Will you be willing to swear to a judge that you will instruct George in the Hispanic culture?"

"We will do whatever we need to do."

"Think about your answers. Try not to be glib. This is not going to be easy, and you need to be prepared for every eventuality."

And so, the struggle continued from February until the first of June. On some days, it appeared that winning was the only reasonably expected outcome, i.e., no birth relatives equipped to care for George were found, despite an exhaustive search. His father had returned to Mexico and could not be located. All of George's siblings were in foster care, and no opening appeared there.

When Mary relayed that news, we all relaxed. Then, the very next day, Clare would talk about a lovely Hispanic couple who wanted a baby, and our hearts would plummet.

As promised, Bets, now living with us in Texas due to an illness, prepared for the joint birthday celebration on June 8th. By then, we were aware of the two-day error, but it seemed silly to spoil a perfectly good, shared birthday because of incorrect paperwork. We celebrated on June 8th.

The emotional roller coaster continued until June 10th, when Carla called to share the scheduled court date, June 15th, at one o'clock in afternoon. Then those highs and lows really became a trial and the Dellos' house occupants got little sleep. Over the weekend, Dave and Mary decided that George would be their son with or without the court's sanction. They packed suitcases and made plans to leave the country, just the four of them, in the event the court's decision went against them. Of course, only Mary and Dave were aware of that until well after the court's decision.

Carla instructed them to be at her office at noon to go through the procedure one last time.

"Okay, we've drawn Judge Gaither. He's the best in the Dallas County Family Court. So, we're lucky there."

"Does that mean you think we'll definitely win?"

"Dave, nothing's ever definite when you go into a court of law. It does mean we have a better chance. Just answer whatever questions are asked. Be sure to take your time with the answers. Don't be glib or too sure of yourselves but be sincere."

Once in the courtroom, Judge Gaiter first asked for Clare's report. As expected, she did not favor the adoption, but she had no relatives to offer as an alternative. She didn't even have a specific non-relative in mind. Rather, her total stance was: The Dellos' family is not Hispanic. Therefore, they cannot be the best placement for a Hispanic baby.

Mark stood next in line to speak. He spoke glowingly of how well George had done since he had been with Mary and Dave. When asked if he shared Clare's objection to the adoption, he answered firmly and clearly.

"No, sir. I believe Mr. and Mrs. Dellos will provide the right home for George. I support this adoption."

Then, it was Carla's turn to present Mary and Dave's case. Her presentation was short and powerful.

"Judge, this child," she pointed to George, all smiles in Dave's arms, "came to this couple in the middle of the night. He was naked, drug-addicted and near starvation. Look at him today."

As if on cue, George giggled, and the entire court smiled.

Carla continued, "This child needs to be loved by his parents. Mr. and Mrs. Dellos love this child. Mr. Dellos has enrolled in a language class to learn to speak Spanish. Mr. Dellos has Hispanic co-workers, and he has enlisted their help in becoming familiar with their culture.

"Judge, this couple does not need a child; they have one. This couple does not need George; George needs them. This couple simply loves him and wants to make him a permanent part of their family."

I don't remember much else. The judge asked a few questions of Carla. Then he asked a few questions of Mary and Dave. Finally, he made an eloquent speech, which none of us really heard because we were listening for a ruling. Then we heard:

"As of this day, George Sotos is renamed George David Dellos and is the legally adopted son of Mary Elizabeth and David Dale Dellos."

A shout of joy filled the courtroom, and tears flowed freely.

A middle-of-the-night phone call turned into a stroke of luck! We have opportunities every day to answer someone's needs. Sometimes, it is a smile or a hello; other times, it requires much more.

Our responsibility is to follow our path, our hearts and the still small voice that is always readily available.

CHAPTER TEN
A Vacation for Two

The onslaught of electronics, cellphones, constant news bursts and two jobs melded into one, create a world filled with overstressed, overworked and under-pleasured people. It comes as no surprise that some snap and behave in such unseemly ways!

We need to daydream and take 'back porch vacations' more often. In my experience, there are five written-in-stone rules for taking a mental vacation built-for-two.

> **Rule One:** Turn off the outside world, the television, electronics, and phones. Leave the newspaper unread, and don't answer the door bell.
>
> **Rule Two:** Invite your significant other—or person of your choice—to join you.
>
> **Rule Three:** Pour a couple of cups of coffee, glasses of wine or any favorite beverage. Move to a comfortable place, i.e. the patio, the back porch, the den,

wherever you can be alone and uninterrupted.

Rule Four: Agree to suspend reality in favor of fantasizing your individual dreams.

Rule Five: Take turns.

This last rule is the most difficult one to follow. It requires giving the floor to another's dreams, listening and getting lost in someone else's imagination to the extent of becoming a part of their fantasy.

Add to their fairy-tale world. After all, money is no object, time is there for the taking and you are limited only by your mind's boundaries. The stress, the worries and the artificialness of the world will slide easily from your shoulders as you and your partner take a whirl in a perfect world. Full immersion is the only way to go, and your turn will come.

When time runs out or the sun goes down and you return to the physical world, there're still the kids and those attendant responsibilities. The nine-to-five begins again tomorrow, and it will include the same headaches you left there. The mental, physical and emotional trials have only been set aside for a short respite. The only difference is you.

Your batteries are recharged, and you again see things in the proper perspective. No matter what's happening today, good or bad, it's temporary.

The only thing of value is sharing love with those around us. I've discovered these escapes can be enjoyed with a good friend, a child on a picnic or even a bedridden neighbor. Flights of mental fancy cannot be caged; they are always affordable and may add years to your life.

Take a vacation today with someone you love!

CHAPTER ELEVEN

Coming to Grips with Getting Old

My sixty-fifth birthday did a number on me! I would love to say I celebrated it with gusto because I practiced the philosophy associated with "Age is nothing but a number." That was not the case.

I felt old, well past my prime, and it seemed as if every day brought another reminder of my advancing years. The sixty-fifth of the eighty birthdays I have celebrated took the greatest toll on my normally positive outlook. I suspect everyone suffers such a birthday at least once in their lifetimes—maybe it's number twenty-one or forty or any particular one, depending on their circumstances.

About two months before my sixty-fifth birthday, I received various reminders of my advancing years. One day, I hit the jackpot of old age symbols with two jabs to the left brain before noon, and I hope you will enjoy walking down memory lane with me.

My husband picked up the mail, and, as usual, we sorted it over our mid-afternoon coffee break.

"Hey, Hon, here's something from Social Security for you." He handed me an official-looking envelope.

"Are you sure? I'm not expecting anything. You're the one on Social Security." I laughed as I tore open the envelope. "Geez. What is this? It looks like a print-out of my expected earnings should I apply for Social Security benefits. Why would they send that to me?"

"I suppose because you'll be sixty-five soon."

"Well, I was born in forty-three, so I'm not even eligible for full benefits until next year. Jumping the gun, aren't they?"

"What about Medicare? Don't you need to make some sort of selection there?"

Now I was just a bit annoyed. *Medicare! I work. Why would I need Medicare? Old people are on Medicare, retired people. Not me. I go to work every day.* I didn't bother to answer my husband. I just laid the note aside to read, unobserved, later.

As it turns out, people must choose to enroll in Medicare B when they turn age sixty-five, or decline the invitation and take a chance on losing a later opportunity. I say "take a chance" because there are certain rules, date-sensitive timelines, etc., that must be followed. With my memory seeming to go south more and more every day, I didn't want to leave that to chance. Besides, one can never have too much health insurance. I noted enrollment was allowed anytime within the next sixty days and put the packet in my purse.

Sunday night, I plugged in my cellphone to recharge. It didn't seem to be working, but I reasoned that might be because the battery was not fully charged. By the next morning, it became painfully clear that my cellphone had died. In my business, I need a cellphone. I decided to take the morning off to kill two birds with one stone.

At nine-thirty, I walked to the entrance of AT&T to discover the door locked. An older gentleman sat outside Starbucks at a table next door.

"They don't open until ten. Join me for a cup of coffee?"

"No, thanks. I've got some other errands to run. I'll just come back." *What's wrong with this youthful world? Don't people go to work at a decent hour?*

Rain began falling, adding a little more gray to my already cloudy state of mind. No need for me to check the address of the Social Security Office; I knew exactly where it was. In about fifteen minutes, I exited Elam Road, which I soon discovered was one exit too far. Eventually, I checked in at the Social Security Office, proudly holding the "B-39" number and awaiting my turn. I took advantage of the waiting time to indulge in one of my favorite activities, people-watching.

Checking in was a simple process. When people entered the door, a short walk straight ahead ended at a customer numbering machine. To encourage visitors to walk directly to the machine, a line of chairs formed sort of a hallway leading in the right direction. Above the machine hung a large sign lettered in large print.

IF YOU HAVE AN APPOINTMENT, PLEASE PRESS "0" AND ENTER ON THE KEYPAD THE LAST FOUR DIGITS OF YOUR SOCIAL SECURITY NUMBER. PLEASE BE SEATED AND YOU WILL BE CALLED BY NAME.

***IF YOU DO NOT HAVE AN APPOINTMENT** AND NEED TO APPLY FOR A SOCIAL SECURITY CARD, PLEASE PRESS "1" AND TAKE THE NUMBER*

ASSIGNED. PLEASE BE SEATED AND YOUR NUMBER WILL BE CALLED.

IF YOU DO NOT HAVE AN APPOINTMENT *AND HAVE OTHER BUSINESS, PLEASE PRESS "2" AND TAKE THE NUMBER ASSIGNED. PLEASE BE SEATED AND YOUR NUMBER WILL BE CALLED.*

As I sat there for less than ten minutes, I observed one couple come in and move the chairs to gain access to a help desk to inquire where they should go to check in.

Another gentleman could not locate the number "2" key, even though it was located between the "1" and "3" keys. The white cap on it confused him.

And a third person waited patiently in line, reached the check-in machine, passed it to walk to a booth and requested that she be helped immediately, as she didn't have time to wait.

Finally, I heard "B-39, please come to window five."

I quickly gathered my purse and reported to the appropriate window. We exchanged pleasantries, the clerk checked my ID and asked the nature of my business.

"I want to enroll in Medicare Part B."

"Are you working?"

"Yes."

"Are you aware that you do not have to enroll at this time?"

"Yes."

"Are you aware there is a premium charge for Medicare B?"

"Yes."

"Fine, Ms. Martin. Please take a seat, and you will be called by name to complete the application form."

For forty minutes, I watched people and became depressed as I realized these people were now my peers. Lord knows, I would not want anyone of them to be on my jury panel. A generous fifty percent of them seemed to suffer from the side effects of the awful disease which I apparently now had: Old Age.

Three out of ten entered the last four digits of their Social Security Numbers on the keypad even though they had no appointment.

"M-125, please come to the D window."

An elderly man made his way to the designated spot.

"Do you have an appointment?"

"No."

"Then, sir, you must re-check in."

"What?"

"Sir, if you don't have an appointment, then you need to check-in accordingly."

"What?"

"Sir, what is the nature of your business this morning?" The clerk spoke in a louder tone.

"I need to change my address."

"That can be done on-line."

"What?" The gentlemen leaned in.

"Sir, go back to the front door and check in again. You'll need to press two and wait for a number assignment."

"Well, that's bullshit!"

"Yessir," the attendant answered and continued with her job. "Number A-43?"

The gentleman walked off at a surprisingly steady and strong gait. I watched him press two to get his number and then sit down to wait again.

There were several more "M" calls before I realized so many people did not read the sign that the system actually had assigned "M" for mistake to the incorrect check-in participants.

Many of those waiting misunderstood or did not hear the number called.

"B-51, please come to Window five."

No answer. "B-51, please come to Window five."

No answer. "Last call. B-51. Come to Window five."

At this point, the Help Desk clerk walked among the rows in an attempt to find the person holding the number.

"B-51. Look at your tickets. Are you holding B-51?"

"Oh, that's me. Sorry," a whitehaired elderly man with a cane answered.

"That's okay. Just go up to Window five." The clerk glanced at the ticket. "Wait a minute, sir. Your ticket is B-61. I'm looking for B-51, five-one."

The man sat back down as an elderly woman jumped up.

"Well, why didn't you say so? You young people never enunciate clearly. If you want five-one, then you should say five-one. What window was that?"

"That would be Window five, ma'am."

And so it went as the minutes ticked off the clock.

There were signs reminding people to know their social security numbers and to have picture ID ready for display when they reached the designated windows. Still, some of them began to go through purses the size of suitcases only after reaching the window. To the clerks' credit, they exuded endless patience, never acting annoyed or rude.

I took solace in the fact that I'm not like "those" people. I still have my faculties about me. *Some of these patrons behave as if they don't know sic-em from com'mere. These must be the old people who have let themselves go, who are really the retired ones. Not me, I'm still in good shape. I may be sixty-five, but I'm as sharp as a tack.*

"Olevia Mullen-Martin. Please report to Window three."

Picture ID in hand, I hurried to answer the summons.

"Hello, Ms. Mullen-Martin. May I call you Ms. Martin?"

"Of course."

"Okay. How can I help you?"

"I want to enroll in Medicare Part B."

"Are you still working?"

"Yes."

"Do you understand that you do not have to enroll in Medicare B?"

"Yes."

"Do you understand that Medicare B has a premium to be paid?"

"Yes." I began to lose patience. Her litany was a complete repeat of all the earlier questions. Apparently, this clerk did not understand I was not *one of those people*. I squelched an audible sigh, but I knew the clerk could read the body language. She smiled slightly.

"Okay, Ms. Martin, do you have your birth certificate?"

"No, I didn't know that would be needed."

"Well, let's see if we can use the information, we have here to verify your age. In what town were you born?"

"Tioga."

The clerk just looked at me.

"Oh, I'm sorry. That would be Alexandria."

Still, she said nothing.

"Geez. What's wrong with me? Pineville, Louisiana."

"Bingo." The clerk looked pleased. "What about your name at birth?"

"Olevia Yeager Mullen."

"At birth."

"Olevia Ann Yeager." I tried to smooth it over with a little joke. "Guess sometimes you are married so long it feels as if you've been married since birth." I laughed nervously.

"Oh, how long have you been married?"

"Two years."

"Two years?"

"Two years to my current husband. I was widowed 1-03-06."

"Widowed 06, and you've been married two years?"

"I'm sorry. That date is 1-06-03."

The clerk smiled her most kind smile. "Just slow down, honey. We'll get this done."

God, I am one of them!

We completed the enrollment, and I went back to AT&T.

The welcoming guy looked at my phone, pronounced it "toast" and said I needed an upgrade. Again, I became a number and received instructions to look around at the various phones. I may as well have been a pig asked to choose a silk purse.

Cellphones can be attached to personal computers, have Internet capacity, can transmit video while people are talking and announce the name of your caller. Prices ranged up to better than seven-hundred-dollars—and that included the one-hundred-dollar rebate! I was gobsmacked!

Finally, a young man called my number, and I hastily responded, "Hi. That's me."

"How can I help you?" A kid that looked to me to be about thirteen, but surely must have been in his twenties, smiled and extended his hand. I thought we were going to shake hands, but he simply reached for my number card.

I regained my composure. "My battery won't charge anymore. I might just need a new battery."

That remark seemed to truly amuse him as he reached for my phone.

"No ma'am. I don't think so. How long have you had this phone?"

He actually blew on it as if it were dust covered.

"About three years, I think, but I keep it pretty clean." I chuckled, and he had the decency to look a little embarrassed.

"Okay, Ms. Martin. Let me see. Just guessing, I'd say you use your phone for calling people and maybe an occasional text message. Am I right?"

I so wanted to take the smartass route and say I did my college homework with it as well, that I might need that seven-hundred-dollar model over in the corner. Instead, I nodded.

"Okay, then let's look at the little Sony model here. I got one just like it for my grandfather last week. He loves it."

Maybe I should wear a sign: I'm old. I'm tired. I think I'm coming down with a cold. Don't push me around.

Again, I smiled and nodded. "That'll be fine. I don't have time for all those useless gadgets. I've finally reached the age of contentment. Don't worry, Honey, you'll get there some day, too."

I think God forgives those little white lies!

CHAPTER TWELVE
Follow the String

One of my mom's favorite things to say to me when I complained was, "Grow where you are planted, Olevia. God made a special place, just for you, and that is where He put you."

As a child, I chafed at that directive. I reacted not to what she said, but to what I heard. "Be satisfied. Squelch your ambitions. Don't ask for more."

As I grew older, I began to hear, not only her words, but also the sound of the life she lived. The sound found in honesty, love, compassion; the sound of my mom's life echoed in every person she met. I began to listen, hear, and remember from a deeper spiritual place. Now those words are understood and used as the basis for following a string through the maze of life.

The spot where I've been planted changes often, and I must keep my eye focused on that string wherever it leads.

Today, this hour, this minute is all there is in any life. Everything else is either the future or the past. I face this instant in my life to the best of my ability because the next one will come without any encouragement from me, but it will be altered by what I do now. When my goals are to love all, tolerate differences by searching for common ground, and to create a better atmosphere for everyone sharing my instant, the rewards are abundant. But the Golden Rule does not always work every time for every person.

I watched a story on a TV broadcast, *20-20, Dateline,* or some such show. It happened years ago, and, while I don't remember the broadcaster, I distinctly remember the people portrayed. The show began by telling the background story of a crime committed some twenty years before: a brutally raped woman, whose perpetrator had finally reached the time he could be considered for parole.

The forty-one-year-old inmate had been twenty-one when he committed the rape and incurred the conviction; his mile-long rap sheet reflected a kid dead set on wasting his life, creating havoc and hurt among all he met along the way. Prison appeared to be a turning point where he obtained a college degree—I don't remember in what—and received an appointment to a semi-management position working with other inmates via rehab programs.

Based on what I saw and heard on the show, the man seemed to have bloomed where he planted himself by his actions. The man of today bore little resemblance to the criminal of twenty years ago. The rape victim had difficulty seeing anyone other than the twenty-one-year-old who viciously committed the crime.

The reporter's conversation with the victim went something like this:

"Ms. Brown, what do you think about Mr. Jones' appearance before the parole board?"

"I'll fight to keep that monster in prison."

"I understand he sent you written apologies?"

"Apologies! That doesn't change anything. I can't go before the parole board to get rid of the pain he caused me. I still can't trust anyone, and I have fears I never had before that awful night."

"Can you imagine a day when you would be willing to see Mr. Jones' life sentence commuted or parole granted?

"No. He took something from me that can never be returned. He has no right to freedom, and I'll fight against that freedom as long as I live."

My heart hurt for that woman as the victim of a terrible crime, but more so because she chose to relive the worst day of her life, every day of her life. She drowned in a sea of hurt from which she refused to be rescued by the only person who could rescue her—herself. She could not see that her freedom, her happiness, her joy depended on her ability to forgive. She allowed herself to be imprisoned by a rapist who—if still considered such—was no threat to her. She remained angry and unwilling to offer forgiveness that could unlock a door for the rapist.

More importantly, she remained in a jail of her own making living the yesterday, every day, a jail to which only she held the key—forgiveness.

I think it was Ben Franklin who said, "Anger is never without a reason, but seldom is it a good one."

Everyone controls the key to their personal happiness. God is no respecter of persons, and not one of us can know the circumstances of another. Vows are easier to make than to keep. It's the choice of what vows we make that is most important.

Remembering and recognizing the inability to walk in another's shoes and their inability to walk in ours is the true answer. Judging anyone only by the worst thing they ever did is a trap just as solid as using only the best thing they ever accomplished as the barometer of who they are. The ability to accept that not one person is better or worse than anyone else is a challenge because we look only to the surface.

I am committed to following the string as I live my life and follow my goals. Celebrating life as it happens in the 'instant' where I am and acknowledging that the only person I can change is me. God made a space for me where I am—wherever that is today and wherever it will lead tomorrow. I will grow where I am planted.

Follow the string. Walk through whatever doors open today, without regret for any that close.

Peace must come on a person-by-person basis.

CHAPTER THIRTEEN

What Is the Greatest Evil?

Is there any such thing as the greatest evil? I doubt it, but if so, I would vote for fear. Fear is certainly the most insidious and acceptable source of evil.

Religious beliefs, when unpruned and unchallenged, warp the hearts and minds of otherwise good and kind people. That same fountain of evil produces great love and kindness. The footprints are equally clear, only the teachers and believers are different. It's the zealots on either side, whether teacher or believer, whether good or evil, who muddy the water when it comes to religious tenets.

I choose here to speak from that vantage point. The Jim Joneses or David Koreshes of the world are the exceptions to the mainstream Christian churches on every corner. The violence in Ireland, the ethnic cleansings, the witch burnings, the children's crusade, to name only a few of the historical examples, are the known, the publicized, acts of Christian doctrine horror. Those are the kind we can all agree on are examples of extremism: hate practices. Those are the types we can band together to prevent or circumvent.

It's the other almost invisible, but maybe more Machiavellian, acts performed in the name of God that represent the real and most frightening evil because we ignore them or join in their practice. Two of many malicious hate cancers—racism and homosexuality—are grown in our society by God-fearing Christians. The same model is true for most of the world's religious faiths.

When I was about sixteen years old, my dad gave me a book to read. I cannot remember the name of it now, but I fully recall the importance he placed on its teachings.

"Olevia, this book is based on the Bible. In here, you'll find out why the white race is to be exalted and why the 'n*****' are here to serve."

"What do you mean, Daddy, here to serve?"

"Read the book. God tells us right there in His Word what our responsibilities are. We are burdened with the responsibilities that go with superiority."

I read the book and found the message distasteful, as it mutilated scripture to suggest God-imposed responsibility on white people to take care of black people, keep them in their place and treat them kindly, but as children and servants. Beatings, lynchings, and untold persecution have resulted from this *Christian* teaching and our world suffers from the deeply embedded mistrust between the races. The election of a black American president made a step in the right direction, but the ladder is still tall, and the bigotry is deeply rooted.

****

My youngest daughter married her best friend right out of high school. Denise and Michael had an abiding love and respect for each other, and Michael wanted to be the husband of both their dreams. He had been a high school ROTC member, enlisted in the military, and had tried to be as macho and girl crazy as the next guy.

Within just a few months of their marriage, Michael recognized that he could not lie to himself and to the world. He admitted his sexual orientation, and despite the truth, Denise and Michael continue through today to share a special friendship. He shares our family celebrations because we share a love with each other and are 'family' in the best sense of the word.

What exists, but doesn't touch us individually, can be ignored. I had no real awareness of homosexuals or their plight because it had not rested on my doorstep. Thus, I found it difficult to accept the reactions of many of our relatives and friends.

Peggy and I had lived next door to each other for over twenty years and were close friends. We raised children together, were scout leaders together, and yet her response shocked me. Several months after Michael and Denise divorced, Peggy and I were having coffee.

"Ann, is it true that Denise's husband is queer?"

"Michael is gay. Why?"

"Well, it's just so sad. I wish he would go to Jesus with his sin. He could be saved. Have you tried witnessing to him?"

I was appalled. It had not occurred to me that Michael needed to be saved from being who God created him to be.

Our conversation opened no discussion or opportunity to share thoughts. Peggy's mind had been warped to the extent that one biblical interpretation that branded homosexuality a sin worthy of an eternity in hell. His 'differentness' from what Peggy believed, in her mind, earned him persecution and judgment from the rest of us.

California's Proposition Eight is only one of many mirrors reflecting this *Bible-taught* intolerance. Gays and lesbians, as well as other non-gender specific persons, endure the slights, misplaced torment and fewer rights than the rest of us because of a single-minded explanation of a few Bible verses.

Too many Christians behave badly because God says it's the right thing to do. They don't realize The New Testament fails to reveal what Jesus said about same-sex behavior. The Jewish prophets are silent about homosexuality, and six, maybe seven, of the Bible's one million plus verses even refer to same-sex behavior in any way. None of those verses refer to homosexual orientation as it's widely understood today.

It's been my experience that most people who use the Bible to create havoc, civil unrest or to support intolerance do not study the scriptures deeply. Most depend upon what someone else told them was there, or they look for a specific verse to superficially back their position. As Shakespeare said, "Even the devil can cite scripture for his purpose."

I believe it is incumbent upon believers of every religion to study the scriptures for themselves, with open minds and individual direction as received in prayer, meditation or whatever works for them. The Bible is one map to be used in our journey from the other side, through this world, and again to the other side. The lessons found there can be unique to our personal adventure, while offering the universal truths of hope, faith and love.

None of us should limit our study to one interpretation of anything. We must think for ourselves, and the word of emphasis is "THINK." We need to think, study, and investigate. I am responsible for my thoughts and actions, as you are for yours.

Speak up and defend the essence of your individual belief. Mine is: God is Love. Any action, word or thought that does not meet that smell test does not ring true to my basic understanding of the purpose of this journey.

God is Love, and we each are—in the flesh—children of God; we can only be truly satisfied when we accept our role in life.

CHAPTER FOURTEEN

The Spoon Collection

This story begins in 1977 when my husband and I began a Spoon Collection. We had a few spoons, but the collection became an official hobby with a spoon rack purchased in Denver. As we traveled, we chose spoons to memorialize each experience. The rack showcased spoons from our U.S. travels in addition to the ones we collected on around the world birding trips.

Spoon collecting rules included size, rack-fit and the unbreakable rule that no spoon be displayed unless we chose it personally while visiting the spot. More spoon racks, of varying capacities, were added and graced the walls in our house.

In January 2002, Ronnie and I left Dallas in our Alfa Gold Fifth Wheel and came home in mid-November. Many December hours were devoted to our spoons and racks as we sorted through the new ones to be added to our collection as well as choosing additionally needed racks. When we received an anniversary trip to Australia as a Christmas gift from our children, we imagined collecting spoons to commemorate new memories made.

****

On January 4th, 2003, as Ron and I returned from a weekend of Shreveport casino fun, we talked non-stop about any and everything; dying, along with what comes next, became front and center for a few minutes. Talking about death was not macabre but, on this night, it seemed more serious. It was not scary, just interesting. During the conversation, we made a pact: *Whichever of us landed on the other side first would contact the one left behind with some concrete sign easily read by the survivor.*

We were healthy people planning to live many more years, but life consists of surprises, twists and turns. Two days later, Ronnie died while we walked in a nearby park. A heart attack is written on the death certificate.

Seven days later, at seven a.m. January 11th, 2003, it was till dark, with no chill in the air—a Texas winter day that would burn into my memory and end a difficult week. My brother and I sat in my kitchen, reviewing the eulogy. My sister-in-law and niece were in the living room, talking and drinking coffee. I fought through a fog of disbelief. Ronnie and I had enjoyed every day we had, and I felt incapable of life without him. I remembered a day in Deadwood, South Dakota, when we had become separated. As I searched, running from building to building, I almost panicked. Though I felt foolish, I couldn't disguise my intense relief at seeing him. He understood and held me for a minute, though he did chuckle a bit!

That same horror and terror, multiplied by a million times, devoured my spirit as I faced losing him. I felt life would never be the same. At my lowest point that morning, something hit the floor in the living room. My niece called out, "Aunt Olevia, a spoon fell."

Chill bumps covered my arms as I picked up the fallen spoon, marking our visit years ago to Tombstone, Arizona. Chill bumps appear on my arms now, as I write this, just as they did that day.

Soundlessly, I heard Ronnie clearly. "Ann, I have crossed. The tombstone of my life has been set. We will now travel on a different plane."

Becky said, "Look. Another spoon is moving!"

I looked up to see a spoon, near the top of the rack and nowhere close to the one that had fallen, swinging back and forth. That spoon was the only one moving on the rack. I brought a chair from the kitchen and climbed up to determine what vacation it noted. *Australia? How can that be?*

We had not visited Australia. Australia was our planned 2003 fortieth anniversary trip. Again, Ronnie spoke to me. "Australia is not in our future."

I experienced a peace I had not known that week, and that peace got me through that day and many days since. I still do not know how that Australia spoon happened to be on our spoon rack. My granddaughter had been an exchange student there, but I did not—and still do not—recall her having sent us a spoon.

However, the source of the spoon is of no consequence; the connection changed my life. I have received other contacts, but none clearer than that first hello.

The Spoon Collection hangs on many racks in my house. The memory lives in my mind, as clear today as it was on that day.

CHAPTER FIFTEEN

Memories to Take with You

As I watched the news last night and saw the remains of many towns destroyed by tornadoes, I thought of the people who owned those demolished homes. I wondered if they managed to grab the physical things that were dearest to them.

Of course, pets and family would be topmost in what I would fight to save, but beyond that, I pondered what I would regret most having left behind. My mother's vase is important because it feels like a connection to a time gone by. It has been in our family for eighty years. A glance in its direction provides a linkage to my past, as well as a feeling of an unbreakable bond with life. The vase must be saved. Family photo albums came next; my cell phone is always on my person, so I didn't need to consider it.

My purse is the home of my identity, from driver's license to voter's registration, credit cards, passport, health ID cards, and the list goes on. But all those things, along with my car, can be easily replaced by government records or insurance. No need to waste the time in saving them.

I glanced around at the hundreds of books I own, but only one was truly irreplaceable— My Bird Life List. The information there leads me down so many memory lanes, where I first saw a particular bird, who shared that trip with me, what was the occasion, etc. That tangible book of memories would be sorely missed.

I have several boxes of paper—old newspaper articles, letters written to me by my father, letters between my mom and dad, letters from my brothers and sister, marriage licenses, obituaries, birth certificates, a couple of baby books, etc. Those boxes needed to make it to safety.

As I mentally scanned my home for other items most meaningful, I spotted the two spoons my late husband used to say goodbye to me in 2003; those are a must to be packed.

There are many more tangible items I would truly miss if they were destroyed, but the memories remain mine. That's a complicated thought. The memories are mine; they cannot be destroyed by fire, and they cannot be stolen. That realization alone eliminates most of the material things I consider important, but not the things listed above.

By recognizing the truth of needing tangible proof of some memories in my life, I accept I have a long way to go in my spiritual growth. There will come the time when I am one with all, but not during this earthly life.

Life is always good, and remembering the good times makes it better!

CHAPTER SIXTEEN
Finding Truth

Is the question really whether there is life after death? Or should we ask if there is life after life? Or, perhaps, we should ask, "Is this all there is?"

Many knowledgeable and skilled authors have taken on the subjects, with both clarity and conviction. I have studied works from different points of views, religions and various 'facts' presented as proof. Every seeker should make their own journey to truth, and I invite you to consider my findings.

My conclusion as I write this is: we were alive before we arrived in this incarnation, and we'll still be alive when we leave it. Souls travel in groups as we learn and grow spiritually toward an ultimate reconnection to our Maker. Human relationships change throughout the reincarnations where, in one lifetime, maybe we are the parent, in the next, the child, or maybe an in-law or just a friend.

So, if I am having a problem with a friend and/or a family member, it is better to work it out now because that person is likely to show up again somewhere down the line.

There is a death of the physical body, but that is only the house where my soul and my mind live during the earthly journey. That house is a choice I made before I began this adventure. Prior to arriving on this side, I participated in choosing not only my goals for spiritual growth, but also the forks in the roads I would encounter and the challenges I would face as I work toward my ultimate spiritual perfection.

I am a Christian, and I grew up in a Southern Baptist Church. My faith began on a very narrow basis. Prayer, study, meditation and seeing God at work all over the world has allowed my faith to become more inclusive and broader. This life is meant to be so much more than just waiting for heaven and trying to avoid hell.

We have both heaven and hell right here, today, all around us.

I, like every other person born into this world, began my earthly existence with a completely free will. God allows me to make my own choices. He embodies perfect good, perfect love and compassion. My creator allows me to choose, at every fork in the road, and sometimes I do not choose the road to peace, love or spiritual growth. Sometimes, I choose to indulge my lower human impulses, and I create my own hell right here on earth.

I, like every other human, began in the image of God with all the same characteristics and abilities, much as a single drop of water has the same attributes as the ocean but lacks the power to express it alone. I cannot do it alone. I need God to succeed to the highest degree possible, but that does not translate into being cast into some lake of fire to suffer for eternity for mistakes made.

The only reasonable definition of hell, to me, is the separation of the soul from God. My journey from the day of my creation is one toward reuniting with God. When I pass to the other side from this physical life excursion, time will be provided, as much as I need, to consider the mistakes I've made, the hurts I've imparted to others, the love I've received, shared and given.

In short, a life review, a time of rest, remorse, recovery and reunion will occur when I cross over. My soul will decide if, when and under what circumstances I return for another incarnation and opportunity to further reduce the chasm between my soul and my Creator. Spiritual growth on the other side is slower because there are no forks in the road other than that decision.

I have experienced communication with souls who have passed. During my earthly education, I have been given an opportunity to both express and enjoy love, peace, tolerance, kindness or not. It is my choice. God stands by, ready to forgive, to comfort and to guide. The destination may not truly be up to me, but the journey is, via my free will to choose right or wrong.

I have no photos or videos or recordings of what happens when people die. I have only my beliefs, my prayers and experiences on which to rely.

To have an open mind indicates a willingness, indeed, a desire, to actively search for any evidence that disproves one's beliefs and to weigh any evidence found. An open mind requires listening to others, as well as reading conflicting thoughts and ideas with an effort to understand them.

I am comfortable with my truth based on an open-minded approach to much study, meditation, prayer and experience.

CHAPTER SEVENTEEN

The Boy in the Green Shirt

Several years ago, while visiting my daughter's home, I had the pleasure of seeing what being color-blind, when it comes to the races, really means.

I sat in the backyard watching my five-year-old grandson play with some T-ball friends. One of the kids accidentally threw a ball over the fence into a neighbor's yard, and George came running over to me.

"Grandma, can you get the ball for us?"

"Yeah, sure. Whose ball, is it?"

"It's Jerry's"

"Who's Jerry?"

"He's the boy in the green shirt."

George's playmates were five other little boys; four of them were Caucasian and one was African

American, Jerry. The primary difference George saw between Jerry and his other four friends was a green shirt. It struck me then, and I still think about it. I have told that story hundreds of times.

George's words that day personified what I want for all my grandchildren: the realization that there is only one race, the human race, and it comes in many colors, with many religions, many customs and all with the same needs for love, forgiveness, compassion and honesty.

I wish for my grandchildren, great-grandchildren and all children to realize that each of them is 'enough' in and of themselves. I wish for them the wisdom to look for that completeness in every other person, to search for the common ground. For it is only that common ground that can save our world, both collectively and individually.

Watching my children and my grandchildren exhibit this wisdom and share it with their own children is among my greatest blessings.

There is hope. I have seen it and continue to see it.

CHAPTER EIGHTEEN
Laughter Heals

It was October, 1963; I was nine months married after a brief courtship and expecting our first child in three months.

On this gorgeous Sunday, Ron and I were on our way home from a weekend of visiting family. As we drove through Shreveport, I told Ronnie stories of past days spent at the Shreveport State Fair; it happened to be in full swing that day. I suggested we stop for a while.

"Ann, I don't get paid until Friday. We don't have any money to spend at a Fair."

"I didn't say anything about spending money. I just want to walk around and look at stuff. There's a lot of free stuff. Besides, I think I need to exercise a little bit."

"Are you uncomfortable? Should I stop for a few minutes?"

"Let's do that. I think it is only fifty cents to get in. I don't want to do any of the rides any way.

Maybe just go into the buildings, collect some free stuff and look around."

I knew I had won the battle when Ronnie turned at the next corner. Once inside the Fair gates, we walked together for a little while. We went through the tents filled with pies, jellies and other homemade items, taking advantage of all the free samples. Then Ronnie decided to take a detour.

"Listen, if you don't mind, I'm going over to the car show."

"No, not at all. Go. I'm just going to wander around here for a little while. Meet at the gate in an hour?"

"Do you need any money?" he asked.

"No. I've got the ten dollars Daddy gave me to cover the cost of the gas home. Besides, I'm not going to spend any money."

Ronnie had disappeared from sight only moments before I decided a walk down the mid-way could not hurt anything. Carnival hucksters shouting out in their sing-song way carry a certain addictive quality—at least for me. I stopped to watch one of the barkers.

"Step up. Four darts for only a dollar. Burst three Balloons. Take home a teddy bear. Anybody can do it. Step up. Get your teddy bear. Hey, mister, get your little lady a teddy bear."

He stopped the singsong for a moment, threw three darts, and hit three balloons.

"Look at that, ladies and gentlemen! I won the big one, a Teddy Bear the size of that little lady over there."

He held up a large stuffed animal. "But I have a tent full. You, sir. Come over here and win one for your lady friend. She wants one; doncha, Honey?"

I smiled and wandered on down the Midway, stopping to watch the crowds and the barkers. I even looked at the world's most tattooed man. I slowly wandered from one tent to the next. Then I saw a game that looked winnable to me. All one had to do was throw dimes and have them land on one of several plates stacked in the center. When all dimes landed in plates the prize was double your bet. How difficult could that be?

I handed over a dollar and only managed to get three dimes to stay in dishes, so I stopped for a few minutes to watch the barker again as he demonstrated how to launch the dimes so they would land flat. *Okay, I've got it now*, I thought, and I handed over another dollar. I did better: five dimes landed in plates.

Another review of the barker's technique, another dollar and another failure. When I was five dollars in, I started to realize I might be at the point of no return. The huckster, being good at his job, spotted my hesitancy.

"Ma'am, you're gettin' it. I'm going to make an exception for you."

He then gave a little speech to the crowd watching me lose all my money. "This young lady is about to place her bet of five dollars. When all ten dimes land in plates, she will get her five dollars back, plus ten more. That's fifteen dollars"

He turned to me. "What do you think, ma'am? What about fifteen dollars when you started with ten?"

"I'll do it." No hesitation on my part.

I handed over my last five dollars and he gave me ten dimes. The crowd moved in closer to watch this foolish, pregnant lady throw away her last five dollars. The first five dimes landed on plates, no problem. Dime number six slid off to the side.

The huckster spoke up: "That's okay, ma'am, get nine in and I'll give your money back, ten dollars."

The next two landed solidly, but number nine missed the mark. Now, I am shaking as I realize I've lost all my money, after promising my husband of less than one year that I would not be spending any money.

Again, the barker spoke, "Two misses. That's not too bad. Get number ten in there and it's five dollars back in your pocket."

Number ten missed the mark, and I burst into tears. The crowd seemed to sympathize with me, and there was a little chatter. A nearby policeman saw the commotion and came over.

"What's wrong, ma'am? Are you okay?"

"I lost all of my money, and I don't know what to do," I said between sobs.

The policeman turned to the Carnival barker. "How much did she lose?"

"Ten dollars. Fair and square, sir."

"Give her back five dollars."

The barker did not protest as he handed me five dollars, and I thanked him and the policeman. Some in the crowd clapped as I headed quickly for the fair gates.

I saw Ronnie in the distance and began to create stories in my mind to cover the five-dollar loss and considered never mentioning it. But our relationship would not allow anything but the truth and transparency. I blurted out my story the minute I got close enough.

"I lost all our money. I'm sorry. I don't know why I did it. Please don't be mad."

"What are you talking about, Ann?"

Tears filled my eyes until Ronnie began to laugh. At that point, I may have embellished the story a little as I described the barker, the crowd, my performance and the policeman. What could have been an awful day became a treasured memory.

I learned many lessons that day, but the two important ones allowed my marriage to develop into forty years of peace and love.

Shared laughter heals wounds, and my husband loved me, imperfect as I might be!

CHAPTER NINETEEN
A Work in Progress

I had not been married to my late husband for long before I observed one of his "self-check" sessions. He sat with paper and pencil, scribbled some words for a few minutes, then crushed the paper, threw it away and went about his business. I felt puzzled.

"What's the deal, Randall? What are you doing?"

"A self-check."

"A what?"

"Sometimes I have a day that I'm not sure my behavior matched my intentions. So, I list those intentions, think about the circumstances and either check them off as accomplished or remind myself to be more careful in the future. Then I toss the concern in the trash."

"I don't understand."

"Suppose I had a run-in with a waitress today or a disagreement with my daughter or whatever, I might still be upset tonight. Rather than stew about it, I sit down and list my objectives. They always include compassion, patience and understanding, along with getting my point across. By taking a second hard look, I can see both my failures and my successes. The tension is gone, and maybe I learned something."

I stared at him with wide eyes.

He laughed. "You think I am crazy, don't you? I used to have quite a temper, but it never seemed as if I won many battles, and I was always upset with something or someone. An old boss at TXU told me about 'self-checks'. I've just gotten into the habit over the years."

"No, I don't think you are crazy, and you're probably the most patient man I've ever met. Maybe they work."

That scene came to mind, recently, as I sat on the patio, sipping a glass of wine and considering my life. I am certainly happy, healthy, financially okay and I have a super family. But is that all I wanted in life? Have I done my best in all areas?"

I decided to do a 'self-check'. I ran down a mental list of personal goals to determine the ones accomplished and the ones left needing attention. I am not talking about career goals or even family goals—too late for that. Either they have been reached, or they won't be.

Disappointments and a few challenges have provided opportunities for growth and for learning. I've experienced times of great joy and times of great sadness. That is life; that is the path I chose to walk. Oftentimes, it feels as if I have no control over the circumstances in which I find myself.

My thoughts centered around personal attributes, the ones I will likely face when I meet my Maker. So, I pulled out my own mental list of hopes and dreams as to who I wanted to be. I've been blessed with eighty years to reach my goals, and that list allowed me to determine my success and the areas requiring some attention. To the best of my ability, I held myself up against the character traits I wanted and those I exhibited.

I pulled out my compassion and tolerance compass and found it slightly off north. I found too much elbow room between honesty and integrity. I discovered that forgiveness—including forgiveness of myself—had slid a little to the right. Too much of the time originally allotted to the "thank you" jurisdiction had been claimed by the "I want" department. Sometimes the opportunities to be kind were ignored as I set compassion aside for expediency.

As I worked through my list, I was reminded of my favorite Robert Burns' poem *To a Louse* and the lines I love so much:

> *O wad some Power the giftie gie us*
> *To see oursels as ithers see us!*
> *It wad from many a blunder free us.*

My conclusion: I am happy, but I can never be totally satisfied because I am a work in progress. Being unsatisfied, but constantly working toward being a better person is my definition of satisfaction.

Reaching a goal of perfection does not happen on this side, but working toward it creates a satisfying journey.

CHAPTER TWENTY
Some of My Favorite Thoughts

For you to consider:

> Time does not heal wounds, but it allows those wounds to become a buried treasure of memories—memories to be taken out, enjoyed as often as desired and again safely stored away.

> Saying, "I know how you feel. I've been there," is a lie, a well-meaning one, but a lie, nonetheless. No one has walked in someone else's shoes, and no one has walked in mine.

> The concept of being alone is a conundrum. The people whom I have met and learned to love over my lifetime can never cease to be a part of me, and I am a part of them. All energy is eternal and forever connected.

If there is nothing nice to be said, then just be quiet.

When faced with a choice, the decision is already made. Be still, listen to and follow the small still voice always available within.

Life is always good.

Printed in the USA
CPSIA information can be obtained
at www.ICGtesting.com
LVHW010808081024
793246LV00002B/36